MW00478726

Contents

Celebrate Series Overview

The *Celebrate Matthew* DVD and participant guide are part of a series of studies aimed to help people study and apply God's Word and experience life transformation. Sessions are designed to be used in small groups but can easily be adapted for individual study.

The DVDs in this series feature the Bible teaching of Pastor Keith Loy. In each study, Pastor Loy will walk you through a book or books from the Bible, with a focus on helping you apply what you learn in a practical way.

Each participant guide contains study notes, as well as additional material to help you process and apply the tea-ching on the DVD. These include ideas for group sharing, connecting, and discussing, as well as action steps you can follow to implement your learning. You'll also find helpful instructions and guidelines for those who are facilitating small groups.

As you celebrate and study the Word, whether individually or in a group, may God richly bless your life and help you grow in knowledge and obedience to our Lord Jesus Christ.

Celebrate Matthew

participant guide

wesleyan
publishing
house

Indianapolis, Indiana

Copyright © 2012 by Wesleyan Publishing House
Published by Wesleyan Publishing House
Indianapolis, Indiana 46250
Printed in the United States of America
ISBN: 978-0-89827-577-3

Writer: Kevin Riggs

Study Preview

Immediately following his baptism, Jesus was led into the desert to fast and pray and be tempted by Satan (Matt. 3:13—4:11). After this encounter, Jesus began his public ministry by traveling through Galilee preaching, teaching, calling his disciples, and healing the sick (4:12–25). Tired and wanting to get away from the crowds to spend time alone with his disciples, Jesus went up on a mountainside. But the crowds followed, so he sat down and began teaching.

Jesus was a master teacher. He was the prince of preachers and the rabbi of rabbis. People commented, "He taught as one who had authority, and not as their teachers of the law" (Matt. 7:29); and, "When the crowds heard this, they were astonished at his teaching" (22:33).

Jesus' greatest sermon, called the Sermon on the Mount, is recorded in Matthew 5–7. This sermon was really a series of short talks on several different topics. Jesus began with an ethic that has come to be known as the Beatitudes. This ethic describes life in the kingdom of God (5:3–12). From there he discussed a disciple's influence in the world, describing it as salt and light (5:13–16); and then he went into a lengthy discussion about obedience to the spirit of the law, not simply the letter of the law (5:17–48). In the middle part of the sermon, he discussed giving to the needy, prayer, fasting, priorities, and worrying (6:1–34). Jesus wrapped up his sermon by warning against judging other people, being persistent in prayer, and making sure you are on the right path (7:1–23). Finally, he concluded with one of his more familiar parables—the wise man and the foolish man (7:24–29).

Jesus' main audience for this sermon was his disciples, but since crowds were following him everywhere, they listened as "he went up on a mountainside and sat down [with his disciples] . . . and he began to teach them" (5:1–2).

It is an incredible sermon and needs to be read again and again.

In this DVD study of the Sermon on the Mount, you will:

- gain an understanding of the type of lifestyle expected of a disciple of Jesus;
- be strengthened in your walk with Christ as you are reminded how much Jesus loves and cares for you; and
- be challenged to build your life on the rock of obedience to Jesus' teaching.

As you work your way through these twelve sessions individually or as a group, may you be encouraged as you "seek first his kingdom and his righteousness" (6:33).

Guidelines for Group Facilitators

This DVD Bible study is designed as a plug-and-play small group experience, with little or no preparation necessary prior to each session. However, you'll find it helpful for your group to have a facilitator, someone who will manage details and guide the group's experience. Here are some helpful tips for those who serve as group facilitators.

SET THE ATMOSPHERE

Small groups should be casual, welcoming, and inclusive. Arrange a meeting place where people will feel comfortable and relaxed. Most often, this will be a group member's home, but it could also be a room in your church building that is specially equipped for this kind of meeting. Providing coffee, other beverages, and snacks can also contribute to a relaxed atmosphere.

ENCOURAGE PARTICIPATION

Make sure everyone has the opportunity to participate fully in your group. Each week, invite different people to pray, read, or provide refreshments. Also, be ready to give instructions like, "This time let's hear from someone who hasn't spoken up yet," or "Jason, I'm wondering what you're thinking about this. Anything you'd like to share?"

KEEP ON SCHEDULE

This DVD Bible study is designed to take no more than ninety minutes for each session. Here is a typical schedule:

Welcome and Prayer	5 minutes
Share	10 minutes
Connect	15–20 minutes
Discover	10 minutes
Discuss	25–30 minutes
Implement	5–10 minutes
Wrap Up	5 minutes

As facilitator, guide your group through each step of the process and make sure they stay on track and on schedule.

Try to keep your meetings as positive as possible. Establish ground rules early so that each person in your group is treated with kindness and respect.

Being a group facilitator does require a bit of extra time, but your servant leadership can make a big difference in the overall experience of the group.

Attitudes That Should Be, Part 1

MATTHEW 5:1–5

WELCOME and PRAYER
(5 minutes)

SHARE
(10 minutes)

Take turns sharing what you hope to gain from this experience.

CONNECT
15–20 minutes)

Has anyone ever given you "attitude"? In most cases when someone gives you attitude, they are a little snarky, crabby, or petulant. To say someone has given you attitude is not a compliment.

However, in Jesus' most famous sermon, the Sermon on the Mount, he outlined attitudes we are to have, and attitudes we are to give others. As a

The mountain from which Jesus preached his most famous sermon is not identified in the Gospels. For many scholars, this oversight is intentional and significant. The exact location is not important because a parallel is being made between Jesus' words here, and the covenant of law Moses received. The first covenant (Law) was received by Moses while he was on a mountain, and now Jesus was giving a new covenant (grace) from a mountain. The Beatitudes are for the Christians what the Ten Commandments were to the Israelites.

person displays these attitudes, Jesus promised they will be blessed. These attitudes are more commonly known as the Beatitudes. For followers of Jesus, these are attitudes that should be common in our lives.

Facilitator: Invite group members to participate in the following discussion.

What three words would you use to describe the attitudes Christians should have? Do words like *gratefulness*, *thankfulness*, or *forgiveness* come to mind? What about *grace*, *joy*, and *love*? There is a good chance if you asked one hundred Christians to describe their Christian lives in three words you would never hear the words *brokenness*, *sorrow*, and *meekness*. But these are the first three attitudes Jesus said should be in our lives.

DISCOVER
(10 minutes)

Complete the study notes as you watch the DVD together.

The Sermon on the Mount has been called anything from
_____ Christianity to Jesus' great
_____. The sermon remains today as a lasting
source of _____ for anyone who professes to be
a follower of Jesus. The sermon deals solely with the
Christian _____ and how a Christian is to live that
life out—in _____, _____, and _____.
In this first session, we are going to look at those famed
beatitudes—those _____ that should _____—if
we're going to truly be like Christ.

The first attitude that should be, and the first step to
"blessedness" is our _____ of our
_____ (v. 3). To be broken means we realize
we are _____; we are
_____ without him.
God dwells with the person whose
heart is _____.

> The idea of being
> blessed is closely
> related to the Hebrew
> idea of shalom,
> meaning peace.

The second attitude that should be
(v. 4) is a complement to the first.
The first attitude is _____; the second
attitude is _____ (grief over our sin).
We're much quicker to _____, make
excuses, and _____ our sins.

The third attitude is meekness (v. 5). These first three Beatitudes must be seen as one. If people _____ their need of Christ, and are truly _____ for their sins, then it should result in a humbled, gentle spirit.

DISCUSS
(25–30 minutes)

The central message of Jesus was, "Repent, for the kingdom of heaven is near" (Matt. 4:17). After the first beatitude, Jesus said, "Theirs is the kingdom of heaven" (5:3). With Jesus came the kingdom of heaven. By living a life characterized by the Beatitudes, Jesus' followers are giving the world a glimpse of life in God's kingdom.

1. In the context of Matthew 5:1–5, what do you think it means to be "blessed"? In what ways do you feel you have been blessed?

2. What do you think it means to be "poor in spirit"? How does your answer compare to what Jesus said in John 15:5 and with what Paul said in Romans 7:18? In what ways do you think blessings come to a person who is poor in spirit?

3. The DVD states the implication of Matthew 5:4 is to be sorry for our sins. Why do you think it is important that we truly mourn over our wrongdoing? How does a person show he or she is sorry for his or her sins? Can a person repent without being sorry? What other meanings might this verse have?

4. What comes to your mind when you hear the words *meek* or *meekness*? How, and in what ways, can you

show meekness in your everyday life? What do you think it means to say the "meek will inherit the earth"? How is that possible?

5. How does what Jesus said in Matthew 5:1–5 compare with what the apostle Paul said in Colossians 3:12–14?

IMPLEMENT
(5–10 minutes)

Choose at least one activity to do before the next session. Tell one other person which item you chose.

1. On an index card, write the words *brokenness*, *sorrow*, and *meekness*. Carry the card with you over the next several days. Periodically, take out the card and meditate on what these three words mean to your Christian walk.

2. Take some time to write out a confessional prayer, asking God to forgive you of specific sins. As a symbol of that forgiveness, shred the piece of paper.

3. Set a goal of memorizing Matthew 5:3–10. Share this goal with someone in your group for encouragement and accountability.

4. Find someone in your group you can become a prayer partner with during this study. Share phone numbers and e-mail addresses, as well as prayer requests.

WRAP UP

(5 minutes)

Brokenness, sorrow, and meekness are all attitudes that should be in our lives as disciples of Jesus. But there are more! In addition to these attitudes, we need to add desire, mercy, purity, peace, and even persecution. The power to live this life, and the promise of blessings come from God. We will finish this topic in the next session.

Attitudes That Should Be, Part 2

MATTHEW 5:6–12

WELCOME and PRAYER
(5 minutes)

SHARE
(10 minutes)

*Take turns sharing what you learned
from applying the last session.*

CONNECT
15–20 minutes)

At some point, every motivational speaker has said, "Your attitude determines your altitude." Another favorite is, "You can't control what happens to you, but you can control how you respond to what happens to you." As good as those quotes are, and as true as they are, Jesus' words about attitudes are better and truer.

> *The basic idea behind righteousness (Matt. 5:6) is doing what is right at all times and in all circumstances and includes justice, ethics, and morality.*

Jesus wasn't a motivational speaker; he was the Messiah. In the Sermon on the Mount, Jesus wasn't describing steps to success; rather, he was explaining what it meant to be his disciples (and still means today). He was describing life in God's kingdom. You entered God's kingdom the moment you confessed Jesus as Lord, and so life in the kingdom begins at that moment as well.

Facilitator: Invite group members to participate in the following discussion.

Take out a piece of paper and rank yourself on a scale of one to ten on the following statements: (1) Since we last met, I have demonstrated a broken spirit; (2) over the last several days, I have expressed sorrow over my sinfulness; (3) I am the meekest person I know.

How did you do? If you scored really high, you may need to take another look at the third statement.

DISCOVER
(10 minutes)

Complete the study notes as you watch the DVD together.

Attitude number four is desiring God (v. 6). The word *hunger* means to "_____," and the word *thirst* means to "_____ _____ _____." We hunger and thirst for Christ's righteousness. Those who really _____ God have this longing to really _____ in God.

Our next attitude is mercy (v. 7). This is the biblical principle of _____ and _____. I like to put it this way: _____ affects our person and then _____ it; _____ affects our character and then _____ it. Because we _____ forever grateful, we _____ forever grateful.

The next attitude is purity (v. 8). Purity does not imply sinlessness. Purity is not a destination, but a _____. We're quick to _____, quick to _____ our wrongs, quick to _____, and quick to _____.

Our next attitude is peacemaker (v. 9). When things are _____ among the family of God, we are to _____ toward them, making them _____.

Another word for "filled" (Matt. 5:6) is satisfied. *Those who pursue righteousness will live a life of satisfaction.*

The final attitude is persecution (v. 10). Every time we lift up the _____, there will be some who will grow _____. If we call ourselves Christians, _____ will be a part. We're not trying to be a _____, but rather a _____.

DISCUSS
(25–30 minutes)

1. Eight attitudes make up the Beatitudes. In Galatians 5:22–23, Paul listed nine things he called the fruit of the Spirit. What are the parallels between the Beatitudes and the fruit of the Spirit? Which Beatitudes do you think could be paired with which fruit?

2. What do you think it means to "hunger and thirst for righteousness?" Compare your answer with what Jesus said in John 4:13–14, 32–34.

> *To receive and give mercy includes both forgiveness and compassion. We have been forgiven of our guilt, and we are to forgive others their guilt. God has extended compassion to us who are suffering and in need, so we are to extend compassion to others.*

3. On the DVD it was stated, "Grace affects our person and then saves it. Mercy affects our character and then changes it." What do you think that statement means? How would you explain that statement to someone else?

4. What is the principle behind Jesus admonishing us to be "pure in heart"?

5. When difficulties and disagreements arise at work, home, and in the church, how can a disciple of Christ be a peacemaker?

6. How, and in what ways, can persecution be a blessing? Compare what Jesus said about persecution in Matthew 5:10–12 with what the writer of Hebrews says in Hebrews 11.

IMPLEMENT
(5–10 minutes)

Choose at least one activity to do before the next session. Tell one other person which item you chose.

1. Draw two columns on a piece of paper. In one column, list the eight Beatitudes. In the other column, list the nine characteristics of the fruit of the Spirit. Draw a line between the beatitude and the fruit that most parallels the beatitude.

2. Do an Internet search for the prayer of St. Francis of Assisi, and make that your prayer for the next several days.

> *To be "pure in heart" (Matt. 5:8) can have two meanings: First, it can refer to moral (inward) purity and not simply outward actions; second, it can refer to being single-minded and focused. Both meanings fit the context.*

3. Do an Internet search for "persecuted Christians," and commit to developing the habit of praying for the persecuted church on a regular basis.

4. If you have not found a prayer partner in your group, do so, and share prayer requests with him or her. Don't forget to exchange contact information.

WRAP UP
(5 minutes)

Have you ever heard the saying that some Christians are so heavenly minded that they're no earthly good? It shouldn't be that way! If you have placed your faith in Christ and if you are allowing him to develop the Beatitudes in your life, you will influence those around you. You will make a difference. Being salt and light is the topic of the next session.

It is no accident that Jesus follows being a peacemaker (Matt. 5:9) with being persecuted (vv. 10–12). The world does not always welcome people who stand up for what is right.

Salt and Light

MATTHEW 5:13–16

WELCOME and PRAYER
(5 minutes)

SHARE
(10 minutes)

*Take turns sharing what you learned
from applying the last session.*

CONNECT
15–20 minutes)

Jesus came to bring the kingdom of God into the present world. A person who professes faith in Christ is required to impact his or her surroundings. Jesus wants to change you and then use you to change your culture.

Do you think your culture is too corrupt to change? Well, salt doesn't cure the corruption that has already taken place, but it does keep the corruption from spreading any further.

Do you think your culture is too dark to change? Well, the smallest amount of light will dispel the darkest of night.

The salt Jesus referred to was not the same as our table salt. Our table salt is manufactured. Salt in the Bible was a natural resource, fathered from places like the Dead Sea. When our salt loses its flavor, it evaporates. When biblical salt no longer had flavor, it was thrown outside and used like gravel, "thrown out and trampled by men" (Matt. 5:13).

You can make a difference! You will make a difference as you live a life of salt and light.

Facilitator: Invite group members to participate in the following discussion.

When you hear the analogy of salt and light, what comes to your mind? In what ways are salt and light similar? In what ways do salt and light differ? How would you explain to another person what it means to be salt and light? Who is someone you know who has been a wonderful example of what it means to be salt and light?

DISCOVER
(10 minutes)

Complete the study notes as you watch the DVD together.

Jesus said there are two ways we are to impact our world. He told us we are to be _____ and _____.

Salt is mentioned first (v. 13). Salt _____,
adds _____, and brings _____
to that which it encounters. Salt _____ things,
and it only takes a _____ to flavor the entire pot.

The second thing Jesus calls us to be is _____
(vv. 14–16). In the same way light was meant to _____,
so the Christian life is to be _____ for all to see.
_____ is expelled by light; light serves as a
_____; and light is _____ to the eye. The
power of light—a source of _____ that we're to be.
The question is: Are you being God's _____ in this
_____ world? Light is to
be _____. There is no such
thing as a _____ Christian.

> In Jesus' day, lamps were small and made of clay. Lamps had a reservoir to store oil and a spout on one end for the wick. Very little light was provided by the lamps, and so, in the home, they would be placed up high, on a lamp stand, to ensure maximum illumination.

Salt, meaning how we are to live—our _____.
Light, meaning what we do—our _____.

Here is the reality: If we are not _____ them, then we really have no right to be _____ them.

DISCUSS
(25–30 minutes)

1. Why do you think Jesus used salt as an analogy for the Christian life? In what ways can Christians be salt?

2. If you were to use an analogy besides salt, what would it be? How would you finish this sentence: "As a follower of Jesus Christ, you are the _____ of the earth; you are the _____ of the world"? Explain your answer.

3. In what ways can a Christian lose his or her influence or "saltiness" in the world? How can you avoid this from happening to you?

> The bowls referred to in Matthew 5:15 were measuring bowls that were also used to extinguish the flames of a lamp.

4. What do you think it means to be the "light of the world"? What are the characteristics of light that should also be characteristics of the Christian life?

5. How do the words of Jesus in Matthew 5:14–16 compare to the words of Paul in Ephesians 5:8–20?

6. In what ways can Christians hide their light under bowls (Matt. 5:15)? What happens when you hide your light? Can you think of an example in your own life when your light was not shinning as brightly as it should have? What did you do to brighten your light?

7. How do you think your "good deeds" (v. 16) can cause people to praise God, instead of praising you?

IMPLEMENT
(5–10 minutes)

Choose at least one activity to do before the next session. Tell one other person which item you chose.

1. Using a Bible dictionary, Bible encyclopedia, or reliable Internet site, research and study salt and its use in biblical days.

2. Spend time in prayer about how you can impact and influence people at work, school, church, and in your family. Be specific.

3. Find a small, clear jar and fill it with gravel. Place this jar in a prominent place in your office or home. Let it serve as a reminder that when you lose your saltiness (or influence) the only thing you are good for is gravel for others to walk on.

4. Meet with your prayer partner and share what you are learning in this study.

WRAP UP
(5 minutes)

What's the difference between law and love? Are they different, or are they two sides of the same coin? Jesus did not free us from the law. Instead, he fulfilled the law for us, freeing us from the penalty of the law. It is in the freedom from the punishment of the law that we, out of love, live by the principles behind the law. Law and love are the topics for our next session.

Law and Love, Part 1

MATTHEW 5:17–26

WELCOME and PRAYER
(5 minutes)

SHARE
(10 minutes)

Take turns sharing what you learned from applying the last session.

CONNECT
15–20 minutes)

One day a preschool-aged girl was being disobedient to her mother. The mother told the little girl to go sit in the corner. The little girl went to the corner but refused to sit. Standing defiantly in the corner the mother and girl had a showdown. Mom won, and the girl sat down. She then said to her mother, "I may be sitting on the outside, but I am still standing on the inside!" While obeying the letter of

The Law referred to the first five books of the Old Testament (also known as the Pentateuch). The Prophets included, not only the Prophets with Old Testament books after their names, but all the historical books in the Old Testament as well. The phrase "Law or the Prophets" (Matt. 5:17) was a way of saying the entire Old Testament.

the law, the little girl was lacking in the love behind the law.

Often our approach to God's law is like that little girl's: obeying the letter without understanding the love behind the law.

Facilitator: Invite group members to participate in the following discussion.

The posted speed limit is a law most people have disobeyed. A legalist would never break the law. Other people will break the law without thinking of the reason behind the posted speed. What do you think is the reason behind speed limits? Can you break the speed limit and still be obedient to the principle? Can you obey the speed limit while disobeying the spirit behind the law?

What do you think are the reasons behind God's laws? Can you break God's laws and still be obedient to his principles? Can you obey God's laws but be disobedient to the principles behind his laws?

DISCOVER
(10 minutes)

Complete the study notes as you watch the DVD together.

In this session, we will gain an incredible understanding of God's _____ and _____. We will discover the two work together. It was never God's intention for anything to be _____ by way of law.

God's purpose in giving us the law was not to _____ us, but to _____ us. The law was never meant to be a mere legal _____, but a liberating _____.

As one can see, the law was in his _____ and _____. But it would be in his _____ and through his _____ that he would ultimately fulfill it.

> *By fulfilling the Law, Jesus was saying that all the Old Testament was teaching and proclaiming about God finds its full expression in Jesus.*

Why would Jesus use these religious leaders as his example in which we're to follow? It appears _____. Most of the time, Jesus was chastising them for their _____ practices. The answer lies in the understanding of the _____ of that day. The religious leaders were held in high _____.

Imagine if we were as dedicated as they, and then added a _____ and _____ heart. We would be exactly what Jesus desired.

> The main emphasis in Matthew 5:17–20 is that kingdom living happens from the inside out, not outside in. Followers of Jesus are called to a higher ethical standard than the Pharisees and other religious leaders.

Christ was telling his listeners that _____ to the law must move from an _____ valuation to an _____ authority.

God doesn't want us to get rid of the law, but to _____ it.

DISCUSS
(25–30 minutes)

1. Jesus said he did not come to get rid of the law, but to fulfill it. What do you think he meant by that? In what ways did he fulfill the law? Compare your answer to Romans 2:13 and Galatians 3:13.

2. On the DVD it was stated that God's purpose in giving us the law was not to imprison us, but to empower us. What do you think that means? In what ways does the law imprison us? How does the law empower us?

3. The Ten Commandments are the basis of all the Old Testament laws. Read the Ten Commandments in Exodus 20:1–17. What do you think are the principles behind each commandment? What role do you think God's love plays in his laws?

4. Jesus equated anger with murder (Matt. 5:22). Do you think he really meant that one was as bad as the other? What did Jesus mean with those

words? Compare your answer with what is said in 1 Samuel 16:7 and 1 John 3:15.

5. What do you think Jesus meant by his words in Matthew 5:23–26?

6. How important is reconciliation to you? Jesus said that reconciliation is always your responsibility. Is that fair? Why or why not?

IMPLEMENT
(5–10 minutes)

Choose at least one activity to do before the next session. Tell one other person which item you chose.

1. Discussion question 3 asked you to think about the principles behind the Ten Commandments. On a sheet of paper, write out each commandment (the letter of the law) and what you think the principles are behind each commandment (the love behind the law).

2. Get alone with God and reflect on your relationship with him. Are you keeping God's rules without displaying his love? Are you abusing God's love by not being obedient to his commands? Do you struggle with anger and forgiveness? Journal your thoughts as you think through these issues.

3. Reconciliation was a big part of this session. Is there anyone you need to be reconciled with? Make that

phone call or write that letter seeking forgiveness and reconciliation.

4. Meet with your prayer partner and share praise reports and prayer requests.

WRAP UP
(5 minutes)

In the next session, we will continue to look at what Jesus said about obedience to the law and his examples of fulfilling the law. We will discuss things like adultery, divorce, promises, revenge, and enemies. Work ahead by reading Matthew 5:25–48 for the next session.

Law and Love, Part 2

MATTHEW 5:27–48

WELCOME and PRAYER
(5 minutes)

SHARE
(10 minutes)

*Take turns sharing what you learned
from applying the last session.*

CONNECT
15–20 minutes)

At the heart of most problems is a problem of the heart. This is the point Jesus made in today's passage. A person who keeps the letter of the law but neglects the heart of the law is guilty of breaking the entire law. That's a very high standard of conduct! We are saved by grace and kept by grace, but grace does not give us a license to sin. Quite the contrary! God's grace calls us to a higher ethic than

God's Law. But where God calls, he equips. Through the power of the Holy Spirit (God's grace gift to us), we have the power to live by this higher standard.

Facilitator: Invite group members to participate in the following discussion.

What do you think is the hardest thing about living the Christian life? Why do we find it so difficult to do what we know we should do? Do we make the Christian life more difficult than it needs to be? How can we make sure our hearts are right and our thoughts and actions are in sync with each other?

> *Jesus uses hyperbole in Matthew 5:29–30 to emphasize the importance of marital faithfulness.*

DISCOVER
(10 minutes)

Complete the study notes as you watch the DVD together.

Based on what is said in Matthew 5:29–30, Jesus wasn't encouraging us to go around _____ and _____. But think about the alternative—to having seeing eyes and perfect teeth, yet spend eternity without him. Again, note Jesus' transition from _____ to heart _____.

Jesus' word about divorce in Matthew 5:31–32 has been abused and misused over the years. Jesus wasn't providing anyone with a _____ case for divorce, but rather challenging his audience to asking themselves _____?

Think about it: The Bible describes us as his _____, and if anyone has a right to divorce, it would be him. Yet he would choose to _____ and extend _____ than move on without us.

We need to get back to that day where our word _____ something—where we're high on _____ and _____. Is there a promise you made that you haven't or didn't _____? Is there a vow that you need to go back and make _____?

> Many religious teachers in Jesus' day were interpreting Mosaic law allowing divorce to include almost any reason (Matt. 5:31–32). Thus, divorces were quite common, and Jesus was taking issue with this attitude.

The law of Moses was all about _____ _____, and keeping people from taking the law into their own hands.

If we treat our enemies the same way they treat us, what _____ has Christ really made _____ us?

DISCUSS
(25–30 minutes)

1. Jesus' words in Matthew 5:27–28 are difficult. Do you think he really meant that thinking about adulterous acts is the same as committing adultery? What else could

these verses possibly mean? How does Psalm 101:3 fit into this discussion?

2. Jesus' tough words continue in Matthew 5:29–30. If Jesus did not mean to literally pluck out your eye and cut off your hand, what did he mean? How does what he said here compliment or compare to what he said in verses 27–28?

3. What effects has divorce had on your family? How would you explain what Jesus meant in Matthew 5:31–32 to someone else, especially someone who is thinking about divorce or who has gone through a divorce?

> In biblical days, there were different levels of oaths and different penalties for oath violations. Jesus' admonition that "your 'Yes' be 'Yes,' and your 'No,' 'No'" (Matt. 5:37) was a radical departure from that cultural norm.

4. How important is it to you to keep your word? How important is it to you that others keep their word? Why do you think people do not keep their word?

5. If you were to truly live by Jesus' words in Matthew 5:38–42, how difficult would it be? What changes would you have to make in your life?

6. In what ways do you think you can show love for your enemies?

IMPLEMENT
(5–10 minutes)

Choose at least one activity to do before the next session. Tell one other person which item you chose.

1. In prayer, think through the last few movies you saw, books you read, TV shows you watched, and music you listened to. Ask the Holy Spirit to show you any changes you need to make in this area of your life.

2. In session four you were asked to write out the Ten Commandments and the principles behind each commandment. Review that list and ask yourself if you are keeping the principles behind the Ten Commandments.

> *In ancient times, striking someone on the cheek (Matt. 5:39) was seen as an insult more than an act of violence. Jesus' admonition to turn the other cheek was an admonition to not retaliate to the insult.*

3. Is there anyone you have broken a promise to? Go to that person, and ask forgiveness.

4. Meet with your prayer partner to share praise reports and prayer requests.

WRAP UP
(5 minutes)

Giving. Praying. Forgiving. Every Christian would agree all three of those things are important. However, it's not what you give, but why you give; it's not what you pray, but how you pray; and forgiveness is not an option, but a command. A follower of Jesus is to give, pray, and forgive, not in order to draw attention to themselves, but to draw attention to God. The error of self-righteousness is the topic of our next session.

The Error of Self-Righteousness

MATTHEW 6:1–15

WELCOME and PRAYER
(5 minutes)

SHARE
(10 minutes)

Take turns sharing what you learned from applying the last session.

CONNECT
15–20 minutes)

Giving, praying, and forgiving—all three are important for spiritual growth. All three, however, can also lead to pride, hypocrisy, and self-righteousness. Jesus struggled with the religious leaders of his day, not because they were bad people, but because they thought they were good. They thought because they did good deeds, and their good deeds were recognized by others, that they were more spiritually mature than most people. What they did not understand was that God considers a person's attitude about doing good as much as the action of doing good. Without the proper attitude, good deeds lead to self-righteousness, which leads to hypocrisy, which turns people away from God instead of to God.

Facilitator: Invite group members to participate in the following discussion.

> *The synagogue was the center of life for the Jewish community, serving as a place for school, public meetings, prayer, worship, court, and lodging for travelers. In Jesus' day, most Galilean towns had a synagogue.*

One of the biggest reasons people give for not following Jesus is the hypocrisy they see in the lives of Christians. Do you think this criticism is valid?

Hypocrisy may not be the problem, but a symptom of the problem. The problem is self-righteousness, a sense of self-assurance and piety based on outward good deeds. How would you define self-righteousness?

DISCOVER
(10 minutes)

Complete the study notes as you watch the DVD together.

It seems that more people are living for _____ rather than _____ when it comes to living out their _____. Christianity has become more about the _____ rather than the _____, and this is exactly what Jesus was concerned about with these _____ leaders. As Christians, we are to live for an audience of _____—that One being God. Our relationship _____ him is to be a relationship _____ him. With God, it's always about _____.

Our rewards from God are not based on _____ we give, but _____ we give.

> There are two possible meanings of the trumpets in Matthew 6:2. One is a metaphor like saying, "toot your own horn"; the other is of trumpet-shaped collection boxes that hung in the temple. When people placed coins (especially a large amount of coins) into the boxes, the noise would reverberate across the temple.

Prayer is a powerful _____. We all need to ask ourselves _____ and _____ we pray. Jesus gave us two rules concerning prayer (vv. 6–7). First is the principle of _____—to pray _____. Second, Jesus taught us the principle of _____—to pray _____.

There are two key important reasons to forgive (vv. 14–15). The first is that God has _____ us. The second reason we need to forgive is because the _____ is not good. Unforgiveness always hurts _____ more than _____ _____. _____ can't change anything except _____.

DISCUSS
(25–30 minutes)

1. What do you think Jesus meant by encouraging us to not do good deeds ("acts of righteousness") in such a way as to be seen (Matt. 6:1)? How is it even possible to do what Jesus said? Compare Jesus' words here with his words in Matthew 23:1–7.

Religious Jews prayed publically, usually three times a day, at set times in the morning, afternoon, and evening (Ps. 55:17). These public prayers became more about the show and less about the prayer. This is what Jesus was condemning.

2. In today's Scripture, Jesus said we are to give and pray in secret. Do you think this prohibits any type of public prayers and offerings? Why or why not? Does Jesus' admonition have anything to say about seeking a tax deduction based on charitable giving? Why or why not?

3. If God knows what we need before we need it (Matt. 6:8), why pray at all?

4. What do you think is the most unique, amazing, astounding, or awkward thing about Jesus' model of prayer in Matthew 6:9–13?

5. Why is forgiveness—God's forgiveness of you and your forgiveness of others—so important? How is our desire and ability to forgive others related to God's desire and ability to forgive us?

6. In what ways do you think Jesus' words about forgiveness in verses 14–15 compliment and compare his words in Matthew 5:43–48? Is it easier to forgive an enemy or a friend? Why?

IMPLEMENT
(5–10 minutes)

Choose at least one activity to do before the next session. Tell one other person which item you chose.

1. Make an anonymous donation to your church or favorite charity.

2. If you have never done so, begin keeping a prayer journal with a list of specific prayer requests. Carve out time in your schedule to pray through the journal. When God answers a prayer, note it in your journal.

3. If you have never done so, commit to memorizing the Lord's Prayer in Matthew 6:9–13. Encourage your group to memorize the Lord's Prayer and repeat it together.

4. If you have been holding grudges and refusing to forgive someone, meet him or her or write a letter, and ask or give forgiveness.

5. Meet with your prayer partner and share praise reports and prayer requests.

WRAP UP
(5 minutes)

"He who dies with the most toys wins" is the motto of our materialistic culture. Often we equate material things with the blessings of God. Does Jesus have anything to say about our pursuit of stuff? What should a disciple's attitude be about consumerism? Our attitudes about our treasures is the subject of the next session.

Treasures and Trinkets

MATTHEW 6:19–24

WELCOME and PRAYER
(5 minutes)

SHARE
(10 minutes)

Take turns sharing what you learned from applying the last session.

CONNECT
15–20 minutes)

"Show me your checkbook, and I will tell you what is really important to you." Checkbooks are almost a thing of the past, but those words from a financial advisor years ago still ring true today. A person can talk all day about their priorities, but in reality "where your treasure is, there your heart will be also" (Matt. 6:21). Your money, like a trail of crumbs, leads to what you truly cherish in life.

The phrase, "Do not store up" (Matt. 6:19) is more accurately translated, "Stop storing up." In Jesus' day, just like today, material wealth was often associated with God's blessings, and this is what Jesus was condemning.

What did Jesus have to say about our pursuit of stuff? He didn't condemn wealth or say it was wrong to possess stuff. Jesus did, however, warn us against letting stuff possess us.

Facilitator: Invite group members to participate in the following discussion.

There use to be a popular bumper sticker that read, "He who dies with the most toys wins." Not surprisingly, that bumper sticker was never put on old, beat-up cars. Do you think that bumper sticker adequately describes the materialism of our culture? Why or why not? What are some other sayings or slogans you hear that come out of our culture's desires to pursue stuff?

DISCOVER
(10 minutes)

Complete the study notes as you watch the DVD together.

Since the beginning of humanity, God knew his chief _____ for our hearts would not be the _____; it would be our _____.

There is an irony here: We call our stuff _____ but what's really _____ who? One thing is for certain: The way people use their stuff is definitely an _____ of the _____ of their hearts.

It has become our custom to divide life into the "_____" and the "_____," but Jesus doesn't make such division. He is clear that a right attitude toward wealth is a mark of true _____.

Note the reference in verses 22–23 to having a single eye, which in that day meant a _____ and _____ eye. But an evil eye, one of double vision, was metaphoric, an eye that would be _____ and _____. And it was to this the Pharisees developed their problem. These religious leaders had become _____ to the master of _____. If we are not _____, so can we.

Therefore, we must develop a _____ eye, assuring that God is receiving our _____ attention.

The Bible doesn't _____ wealth. It's not wrong to _____ things. It's just wrong when our things possess _____.

> *The warning in these verses is not against wealth but against greed, envy, and covetousness.*

DISCUSS
(25–30 minutes)

1. How does what Jesus said in Matthew 6:19–21 compare with James 5:1–6? Can you think of any other principles Jesus gave concerning the accumulation of stuff?

2. What is the greatest challenge you face in balancing the need to live a comfortable life and the lure of accumulating more and more stuff? When does wanting to be financially secure cross the line and become greed?

3. How much is enough? How much is too much?

4. What steps can you take to ensure you do not become possessed by your possessions?

5. In what ways does how a person use stuff indicate the condition of that person's heart?

6. What are some "treasures" that can be stored in heaven?

7. Generosity and gratefulness are the antidotes for greed. What steps can you take to build generosity and gratefulness into your life? How can you teach generosity and gratefulness to your children?

8. What do you think Jesus meant by saying, "You cannot serve both God and Money" (Matt. 6:24)? How have you seen that principle work in your life? How do Jesus' words compare to Hebrews 13:5 and 1 Timothy 6:10?

IMPLEMENT
(5–10 minutes)

Choose at least one activity to do before the next session. Tell one other person which item you chose.

1. Make a short list of your priorities. Next, take a close look at where you spent your money last month. Ask yourself: Do my spending habits line up with what I say my priorities are? Pray about what changes need to be made in your financial life.

> *There are two possible interpretations of Matthew 6:22–24: (1) A person trying to focus on both God and money has double vision and therefore no clear direction; or (2) a person focused entirely on the accumulation of things is both spiritually and morally blind. Either interpretation fits the context; the importance of having a single focus on God and the things of God.*

2. If you have never created and lived by a household budget, set a goal to do so. Make an appointment with someone you trust who can help you create a budget.

3. An excellent place for your treasure is your local church. If you have never given regularly to your local church, begin doing so. If you do give regularly, pray about giving an extra offering.

4. Read a book about personal finances from a Christian perspective.

5. Meet with your prayer partner and share praise reports and prayer requests.

WRAP UP
(5 minutes)

Most people know it is wrong and unhealthy to worry. But most of us do worry. Many of us worry about worrying! But worrying about a problem never solved it, and excessive worry is bad for both our spiritual and physical health. Jesus had a lot to say about worry, and that is the topic for the next session.

The World of Worry

MATTHEW 6:25–34

WELCOME and PRAYER
(5 minutes)

SHARE
(10 minutes)

Take turns sharing what you learned from applying the last session.

CONNECT
15–20 minutes)

A military chaplain once drew up a "worry table" based on the different problems people brought to him. He placed their worries into five categories: (1) worries about things that never happened, 40 percent; (2) worries about decisions already made and not changeable, 30 percent; (3) worries about sickness that never came, 12 percent; (4) worries about children and friends, 10 percent; and

(5) worries about real problems, 8 percent. Based on his own antidotal study, the chaplain concluded that 92 percent of people's worries were needless.

Knowing the destructiveness of worrying, why do we worry so much? In this session, Jesus plainly said, "Do not worry about your life" (Matt. 6:25). How much happier would we be if we took his words to heart and put them into practice!

> The United States is a high-income country; first-century Palestine was not. For many people, life was a day-to-day existence; so the situation Jesus described in these verses was very real.

Facilitator: Invite group members to participate in the following discussion.

What are the top five things you worry about? Do you think most people worry about those same things? Why do you think Christians worry when they know God is in control?

There is an old saying that goes, "He [or she] could worry a wart off a frog." What do you think that means? Can you think of some others sayings about worry?

DISCOVER
(10 minutes)

Complete the study notes as you watch the DVD together.

What is it about us that we tend to _____ and _____ over life? So much of life is _____, because so little of life is _____.

Jesus gives us four reasons not to worry: First, worry is
_____. _____ don't worry; _____
don't worry. We're the only thing in all of creation that
worries, and we're God's most _____
creation. Second, worry is _____. Worry is
_____ without _____. Third, worry is
_____. Finally, worry is _____. The
only people who should worry are the _____.

What should we do instead of worry? First, _____.
As long as we live for _____ other than God,
we are going to _____. Second, seek _____
and today only. There are two
days every week that we should
never worry: _____ and
_____. Finally, we
are to seek today, _____.
The _____ of worry is
a lack of _____. Worry
and faith can never live in the
same _____. When

> Jesus' point in
> Matthew 6:26–30 is
> that when we worry,
> we are saying we do
> not trust God because
> we are demonstrating
> less faith than birds
> and flowers.

_____ comes in the front door, _____
goes out the back door.

A principle to live by: If you think it's worth _____
about, then it's probably better to be _____
about it.

DISCUSS
(25–30 minutes)

1. Do you think Jesus really expected us to never worry about anything ever? If that is not what he meant in Matthew 6:25, what did he mean? What are some things you can do to help you worry less?

2. How would you answer Jesus' question in verse 25: "Is not life more important than food, and the body more important than clothes?" Be specific.

3. The DVD stated that worry is weird. In what ways is this true?

4. The DVD stated that worry is worthless. How have you seen this truth in your own life?

> Matthew 6:33 draws the listeners' attention back to Matthew 5:20. Life in God's kingdom is the central theme of Jesus' sermon.

5. The DVD stated that worry is wearisome. How and in what ways do you think worry affects our physical bodies? How does your answer compare to Proverbs 12:25?

6. The DVD stated that worry is worldly. What do you think this means?

7. What do you think it means to seek God's kingdom first and his righteousness? How can a person make sure he or she is seeking God first? How important is it to you to seek God first?

8. Jesus said as we seek him first and his righteousness, "all these things will be given to you as well" (Matt. 6:33). What are the "things" Jesus was referring to? Is this an absolute promise or a conditional one? Why?

IMPLEMENT
(5–10 minutes)

Choose at least one activity to do before the next session. Tell one other person which item you chose.

1. Make a list of the top five things you worry about. Once you have made the list, pray Philippians 4:6 and 1 Peter 5:7 over those worries.

2. Write a poem based on Matthew 6:26–30, using the analogy of the birds of the air and the flowers of the field and how God cares for you.

3. The best thing to do when you are worried is worship. The next time you begin to feel stressed and worried, listen to praise and worship CDs.

4. Memorize Matthew 6:34.

5. Meet with your prayer partner and share praise reports and prayer requests. In addition, share with your prayer partner

> *The emphasis of Matthew 6:33 is that it is not enough for Jesus' disciples (then and now) to refrain from pursuing temporary, physical comforts. A disciple must replace that pursuit with a pursuit that is far more significant. These higher pursuits are examples of "treasures in heaven" (v. 20).*

the five things you worry about the most. Pray specifically over these.

WRAP UP
(5 minutes)

One reason self-righteousness needs to be avoided is because it leads to harshly condemning and criticizing others. As followers of Jesus, we have to be extremely careful about judging others. Jesus said, "Do not judge, or you too will be judged" (Matt. 7:1). Those are great words to live by and the subject of the next session.

You Are Not the Judge

MATTHEW 7:1–6

WELCOME and PRAYER
(5 minutes)

SHARE
(10 minutes)

Take turns sharing what you learned from applying the last session.

CONNECT
15–20 minutes)

That's just wrong! You shouldn't do that! I don't think a person can be a Christian and live like that! I would never do something like that!

Have you ever made statements like these? One of the most difficult things a person can do is make a judgment about something or someone without being judgmental. And even when a person can do so, he or she is still accused of being judgmental. How many times have you said something to someone only to get the reply, "Who are you to judge?"

Are Christians to remain silent on all issues? Can a Christian judge without being judgmental?

Facilitator: Invite group members to participate in the following discussion.

Have you ever been guilty of harshly judging someone else? What happened? Have you ever been accused of being judgmental when that was not your intent? What was the situation? Have you ever received harsh judgment and condemnation from someone else? How did you handle it?

In the context of Matthew 7:1–2, the word judge *carries the idea of "condemnation."*

How can a person stand up for what he or she believes in without being judgmental? Is that even possible?

DISCOVER
(10 minutes)

Complete the study notes as you watch the DVD together.

It is important to note that Jesus' words in verse 1 are _____ a command to be _____ toward any moral injustice, but a _____ against one's _____-_____. Christ is not telling us to avoid evaluating people; he's showing us how.

What Christ is condemning is our criticism toward others that is _____ founded and _____ motivated.

There is a reward in letting _____ be God. So leave things in his hands. He will _____ every score. He will _____ every wrong.

Judge _____ first and help _____ look good before you judge them _____ to make yourself look _____. Remember, _____ begins with _____.

The word translated "measure" (Matt. 7:2) is metron, from where we get the word metric. The idea is of a scale or some other instrument used to calculate weight or distance. Jesus was telling us to be careful in setting a standard so high for others that we cannot live up to it.

Jesus always dealt with people based on their _____, _____ to hear, and _____ condition. The fact is, not everyone is _____ or _____ to hear the good news of God.

Always remember, God has _____ us with his precious truth in his Word, and we must handle it with great _____ and _____.

DISCUSS

(25–30 minutes)

1. How can a person make a moral judgment about something or someone without sounding judgmental? Is it even possible to stand up for something without being accused of being judgmental? Why or why not?

2. What do you think Jesus meant by saying, "With the measure you use, it will be measured to you" (Matt. 7:2)? How does what Jesus said here compare with what he said in Luke 6:37–38?

3. What do you think of Jesus' illustration of sawdust and planks (Matt. 7:3–5)? How would you summarize the principle he was teaching with this illustration?

4. What are some examples of planks people may have in their own eyes that they do not see, while they point out specks in other people's eyes? Did Jesus mean that because of sin in our own lives we should never point out sin in other people's lives? If not, what did he mean?

5. How would you define a hypocrite?

In reflecting on Jesus' illustration of a "speck of sawdust" in someone else's eye compared to a "plank" in your own eyes, don't forget Jesus was a carpenter.

6. What do you think Jesus meant by saying, "Do not give dogs what is sacred; do not throw your pearls to pigs" (Matt. 7:6)?

IMPLEMENT
(5–10 minutes)

Choose at least one activity to do before the next session. Tell one other person which item you chose.

1. If you have wrongly or harshly judged someone, go to him or her and seek forgiveness and reconciliation.

2. If someone has wrongly or harshly judged you, go to him or her and offer forgiveness and reconciliation.

3. Write down any judgmental or condemning statements you have made over the last few months. (If you can't remember any, pray and ask the Holy Spirit to remind you.) Then in prayer ask the Holy Spirit to reveal to you any plank you may have in your eyes and ask forgiveness.

4. Meet with your prayer partner and share praise reports and prayer requests.

> *There were no more detestable animals to ancient Jews than a dog or a pig (Matt. 7:6). Both dogs and pigs were used as metaphors for people who were outside God's covenant community. One possible reason for their revulsion is that both dogs and pigs are scavengers and will feed on dead flesh.*

WRAP UP
(5 minutes)

One of the Christian's main sources of strength is prayer. Most people say they pray and believe in prayer. Prayer is one of the easiest things to do in the world, but is also one of the most difficult. Jesus already showed us how to pray; in the next session, we will discover how to be persistent in our prayers.

Persistent Praying

MATTHEW 7:7–12

WELCOME and PRAYER
(5 minutes)

SHARE
(10 minutes)

Take turns sharing what you learned from applying the last session.

CONNECT
15–20 minutes)

Has your child every worn you out asking for something? When he or she first asked, did you say no but then because of continual begging and pleading, changed your mind and said yes? Often persistence wins the day!

Praying to God is very similar to a child asking his or her parent for something. Prayer is far more than asking, but making requests is a big part of prayer (Phil. 4:6). Whether or not our prayers actually cause God to change his mind from no to yes is a theological debate. God does not give us what we want because we have gotten on his nerves. There is something to be said about persistent prayer.

> To ask means to know your needs and to make your needs known with humility. To seek means to ask in such a way as to pursue God's will. The idea behind knock is persistency.

Facilitator: Invite group members to participate in the following discussion.

Can you think of a time when you wanted something so bad you would not take no for an answer? Have you ever lost something of value? Have you ever knocked on a door so hard your hand hurt?

One thing all three situations—asking, seeking, and knocking—have in common is that you did not quit until you received what you asked for, found what you lost, and received the attention of the person behind the door. What would happen if we approached prayer this way?

DISCOVER
(10 minutes)

Complete the study notes as you watch the DVD together.

Jesus has already given us a model for prayer. Now we will discover his _____ for prayer. Jesus not only invites us to pray, but begs us to come _____, _____, and _____.

If we are going to make it, we have to keep on _____, _____, and _____ at his door. We need to be _____ in prayer.

According to today's passage, it doesn't matter _____ we pray; but rather, it's all about the _____ to whom we are praying.

This passage is not implying a guarantee that what we ask for will be answered according to our _____. God gives only _____ gifts which means, he will answer our prayer according to _____ wants.

Matthew 7:12 is known universally as the _____ _____. It's a principle that says what _____ ordinarily want others to do for them, they should already be _____ toward others.

Bread and fish were staples of the Jewish diet (Matt. 7:9–10). Jesus' first temptation was to turn stone to bread (4:1–4). Jews were prohibited from eating fish without scales (like catfish, Lev. 11). Snakes could resemble fish without scales. No father would trick his child with stones that looked like bread and snakes that looked like fish (or scale-less fish).

You cannot _____ that which you do not _____. Only a follower of Christ can _____ this rule and thereby demonstrate the spiritual change that has come from within.

This Golden Rule is not the sum total of Christian _____, nor is it God's plan for _____. It should only be understood as the _____ of one's _____.

DISCUSS
(25–30 minutes)

1. How does what Jesus said about prayer in Matthew 7:7–8 compare with Ephesians 6:18; 1 Thessalonians 5:17; and Colossians 4:2? What do all those verses have in common? What do they say differently?

> Some form of the Golden Rule is found in most world religions. However, in other religions it is stated negatively: "Don't do to others what you don't want done to you." Jesus turned the rule upside-down by stating it positively.

2. The DVD stated that each key word in Matthew 7:7 was in the present tense, meaning, keep on asking, keep on seeking, and keep on knocking. How does reading verse 7 that way change your understanding of what Jesus was saying?

3. Is Matthew 7:8 an absolute promise that every time we ask we will receive, every time we seek we will find, and every time we knock the door will open? Why or why not?

4. What do you think Jesus meant by comparing bread to stone and fish to snakes (vv. 9–11)? How do you think this illustration applies to prayer?

5. The DVD stated that only a follower of Christ can practice the Golden Rule (v. 12). Do you agree with that assessment? Why or why not? How would you explain the Golden Rule to someone who was not a Christian?

6. How important do you think it is for Christians to live by the Golden Rule? In what ways do you struggle with living by the Golden Rule at home, work, or school?

IMPLEMENT
(5–10 minutes)

Choose at least one activity to do before the next session. Tell one other person which item you chose.

1. Spend more time than usual this week praying over your prayer list, paying special attention to requests that you have been praying about for a long time.

2. Take a few moments to count your blessings, writing them on a piece of paper. After you have counted your blessings, spend time giving thanks to God.

3. Memorize James 1:17.

4. If you feel like you are being mistreated at work, home, or school, make a list of how you would like to be

treated in those situations. Look over that list and ask yourself if you are treating people the way you want to be treated. Pray about the changes you need to make.

5. Meet with your prayer partner and share praise reports and prayer requests.

WRAP UP
(5 minutes)

There are usually two ways to get anywhere: the easy way or the hard way. Most people prefer the easy way, but the easiest way is not always the best way. The easy way may be the convenient way, but it may not be the correct way. Jesus expects us to go down the narrow, less-traveled way. The wide and narrow gates are the subjects of the next session.

The Wide and Narrow Gates

MATTHEW 7:13–23

WELCOME and PRAYER
(5 minutes)

SHARE
(10 minutes)

Take turns sharing what you learned from applying the last session.

CONNECT
15–20 minutes)

Every day we face choices to go one way or the other. Some choices are minor and have no real lasting effect. Other choices are major and what we decide affects every decision afterward. The temptation is to travel the path of least resistance. But sometimes the easy way is not the correct way.

One fork in the road we all face pertains to how to live life. Will we seek God's kingdom (Matt. 6:33) or pursue our own empires? One way has a wide gate and nice paved roads; the other way has a narrow gate and hazardous terrain. The choice we make at this fork in the road affects every decision made afterward.

> The last section of the Sermon on the Mount (Matt. 7:13–29) contains a contrasting pair of four warnings: two paths (vv. 13–14); two trees (vv. 15–20); two claims (vv. 21–23); and two builders (vv. 24–29).

Facilitator: Invite group members to participate in the following discussion.

How many people do you think will be in heaven? What percentage of the population do you think will be there? Will there be more people in heaven or hell? Why? How do you know you will be in heaven and not hell? What is the difference between the narrow gate and the wide gate?

DISCOVER
(10 minutes)

Complete the study notes as you watch the DVD together.

There are two ways to travel: the _____ way or the _____ way. Jesus said we need to _____ another _____.

The life Jesus commanded only comes by a _____, less-traveled way. And such a way requires true, authentic, and inner _____.

This narrow way only heightens the importance of that first step—that _____ _____ of our natural inclinations. The narrow gate is only _____ person wide, and that person is not any of us.

When it comes to the gate, we cannot go _____ it, _____ it, or _____ it; we can only go _____ it.

> The idea of two paths was quite common in Jewish teaching (Matt. 7:13–14). Applications usually centered on one path leading to salvation and the other leading to damnation; or the narrow path meaning the hardships one faces in life that ultimately leads to a broader path of eternal blessing. The first application is the idea here.

Why did Jesus say, "Only a few find it" (v. 14)? First, because of God's _____. If we are honest, we have grown insensitive toward the _____. Second, some people just don't _____; they are ignorant of the _____. Finally, some people just don't _____. They've heard the story before, but have decided there is a better way—_____ way.

We can know the right _____, believe the right doctrine, and obey the right _____, and still be deceived. Satan is truly the _____. He has _____ the minds of so many.

You can only wonder when Christ returns how many _____ Christians will sadly find out they're not truly _____ ones.

Remember, it's not about _____ we do, but _____
we know. It's a _____ relationship, not a
_____ one.

DISCUSS
(25–30 minutes)

1. How do you think Jesus' words about few people going through the narrow gate compare with Peter's words in 2 Peter 3:9 about God wanting everyone to come to repentance?

2. What do you think Jesus meant by saying the wide gate and broad road leads to destruction (Matt. 7:13)?

3. What do you think Jesus meant by saying the narrow gate and narrow road leads to life? Why do you think only a few people choose the narrow road (v. 14)?

In the Old Testament, a false prophet was known by two things: (1) leading people away from God to the worship of false idols, and (2) making prophetic utterances that do not come true.

4. What do you do in your own life to help discern true prophets from false ones? How serious of a problem do you think false prophets are in today's world? What about in today's churches?

5. Jesus said you can tell the difference between true and false prophets by their fruit (v. 16). What do you think he meant by that? What would the differences be between the fruit of a true prophet and the fruit of a false prophet?

6. How do you think people deceive themselves into thinking they are heading for the kingdom of God, only to find out, too late, that they are not heading toward the kingdom of God? (See Matt. 7:21–23.)

IMPLEMENT
(5–10 minutes)

Choose at least one activity to do before the next session. Tell one other person which item you chose.

1. A big part of this session is making sure you have placed your faith in Jesus Christ, choosing the narrow gate. If you have never placed your faith in Jesus or are not sure of your salvation, pray the following prayer, and then let someone know what you have done: "Father, I believe that Jesus is Lord and he died for my sins. I believe you raised him from the dead. I confess my sins to you, asking you to forgive me. I commit my entire life to Jesus and in his name I pray. Amen."

> *In the same way there are false prophets, so there are also false followers (Matt. 7:21–23), and just like the false prophets, the false followers are known by their fruit.*

2. Memorize Galatians 5:22–23, and meditate on the fruit that should be manifested in your life.

3. Meet with your prayer partner and share praise reports and prayer requests.

WRAP UP
(5 minutes)

Few places on earth are as beautiful as the beach. People fantasize of retiring and one day moving near the coast, burying their toes beneath the cool sand, collecting sea shells, and building sandcastles with their grandchildren. But while people dream of living near the sand, no one is foolish enough to build their house on the sand.

In our final session on the Sermon on the Mount, Jesus concluded with an illustration about a wise builder and a foolish builder.

The Wise and Foolish Builders

MATTHEW 7:24–29

WELCOME and PRAYER
(5 minutes)

SHARE
(10 minutes)

*Take turns sharing what you learned
from applying the last session.*

CONNECT
15–20 minutes)

The most important part of any building is the
foundation. Get the foundation wrong, and nothing
in the entire structure will be right. Get the
foundation right, and the most powerful winds
cannot completely destroy the structure. What is
true about buildings is also true about our lives.
Building our lives on the right foundation is of the
utmost importance.

Jesus concluded his most famous sermon with one of his most famous illustrations: the wise builder and the foolish builder, the house on the rock and the house on the sand. As important as the foundation is, the cornerstone of the foundation is even more important. The Bible tells us the cornerstone of a solid foundation is Jesus Christ (Eph. 2:20).

Facilitator: Invite group members to participate in the following discussion.

The mount on which Jesus preached this sermon is unknown. More than likely it overlooked the Sea of Galilee, which would have given Jesus the perfect setting for his final illustration. The sand around the Sea of Galilee would be rock-hard during the summer months, but during the torrential winter rainfalls the sand would become soft. The custom of the day was to dig down into the sand at least ten feet to the bedrock to lay a foundation before you built a house.

There is a children's song about the wise man and the foolish man, based on Matthew 7:24–29. The gist of the song is that the wise man built his house on the rock and when the rains came down and the floods came up, his house stood firm. But the foolish man built his house on the sand and when the rains came down and the floods came up, his house collapsed.

DISCOVER
(10 minutes)

Complete the study notes as you watch the DVD together.

It we're truly following Jesus, obedience to God's Word is
_____. You don't _____ the Bible
into your life, you fit your _____ into the Bible.

_____ qualities are hard to
judge, but storms have their way of
_____ what is really on the
_____. You can't cut corners when
it comes to _____.

> *Twice in this sermon Jesus used his knowledge and experience as a carpenter to illustrate his point (the wise and foolish builder, and the sawdust and plank in the eye).*

Real faith is not built on _____
attendance. Real faith is built on
_____ dependence.

Throughout the Bible, we find many who had fallen
_____ because of _____ times. The
_____ wanted to go back to Egypt (Ex. 14:12),
and Paul wrote that many had _____ him
(2 Tim. 4:10, 16).

Life is _____, and only those who build
upon the Word of God, will be able to _____.
_____ determines the structure.

You must profess with your _____, but you must
believe in your _____. Our words really mean
_____; only God's matter.

We cannot take this sermon lightly, for it was given from the very mouth of God. We have a choice: We can either _____ to it, or be _____ by it.

DISCUSS
(25–30 minutes)

1. What do you think about the statement made on the DVD that you do not fit the Bible into your life; you fit your life into the Bible? What do you think this statement means? Why is it so hard to fit our lives into the Bible?

2. Jesus said the difference between the wise builder and the foolish builder is obedience to God's Word. What do you think is the greatest challenge to being obedient to God's Word? Why is obedience so important?

> *The wise person obeys the teachings of Jesus and can better withstand the storms of life. But the foolish person does not obey Jesus' teachings and is more vulnerable to the storms of life. Obedience is the key difference!*

3. Finish the following sentence: The rain and storms that cause me the most trouble in my Christian walk are . . .

4. Can you think of a different illustration you would use to explain the difference between a wise and foolish person?

5. In what ways do you think the people were amazed at Jesus' teaching (Matt. 7:28)? In what ways do you think Jesus taught with authority (v. 29)?

IMPLEMENT
(5–10 minutes)

Choose at least one activity to do. Tell one other person which item you chose.

1. See if you can find the children's song, "The Wise Man Built His House Upon the Rock" on the Internet and listen to it.

2. Take some time to reflect over the entire study of the Sermon on the Mount, and write down the five most important lessons you learned.

3. Repeat all the Scripture verses you were encouraged to memorize during the course of this study.

4. Meet with your prayer partner and share praise reports and prayer requests. Spend a little extra time in prayer, sharing some of the things you have learned during this study.

WRAP UP
(5 minutes)

Your study of the Sermon on the Mount is over, but your study of God's Word should never end. Commit yourself to continually reading and studying the Bible, and pray about the next group study you do.